STEEL PIER
A New Musical

Lyrics by FRED EBB

Music by JOHN KANDER

WARNER BROS. PUBLICATIONS
Warner Music Group
An AOL Time Warner Company
USA: 15800 NW 48th Avenue, Miami, FL 33014

WARNER/CHAPPELL MUSIC
CANADA: 15800 N.W. 48th AVENUE
MIAMI, FLORIDA 33014
SCANDINAVIA: P.O. BOX 533, VENDEVAGEN 85 B
S-182 15, DANDERYD, SWEDEN
AUSTRALIA: P.O. BOX 353
3 TALAVERA ROAD, NORTH RYDE N.S.W. 2113
ASIA: THE PENINSULA OFFICE TOWER, 12th FLOOR
18 MIDDLE ROAD
TSIM SHA TSUI, KOWLOON, HONG KONG

NUOVA CARISCH
ITALY: VIA CAMPANIA, 12
20098 S. GIULIANO MILANESE (MI)
ZONA INDUSTRIALE SESTO ULTERIANO
SPAIN: MAGALLANES, 25
28015 MADRID
FRANCE: CARISCH MUSICOM,
25, RUE D'HAUTEVILLE, 75010 PARIS

INTERNATIONAL MUSIC PUBLICATIONS LIMITED
ENGLAND: GRIFFIN HOUSE,
161 HAMMERSMITH ROAD, LONDON W6 8BS
GERMANY: MARSTALLSTR. 8, D-80539 MUNCHEN
DENMARK: DANMUSIK, VOGNMAGERGADE 7
DK 1120 KOBENHAVNK

© 2001 WARNER BROS. PUBLICATIONS
All Rights Reserved

Any duplication, adaptation or arrangement of the compositions contained in this collection requires the written consent of the Publisher.
No part of this book may be photocopied or reproduced in any way without permission. Unauthorized uses are an infringement of the U.S. Copyright Act and are punishable by law.

Project Manager: Sy Feldman
Editing by David Loud
Vocal Selections prepared by Paul McKibbins

© 1997 WARNER BROS. PUBLICATIONS
All Rights Reserved

Any duplication, adaptation or arrangement of the compositions
contained in this collection requires the written consent of the Publisher.
No part of this book may be photocopied or reproduced in any way without permission.
Unauthorized uses are an infringement of the U.S. Copyright Act and are punishable by law.

John Kander & Fred Ebb

Theatre: *Flora, the Red Menace; Cabaret; The Happy Time; Zorba; Chicago; 70, Girls, 70; The Act; Woman of the Year; The Rink; And the World Goes 'Round—The Kander & Ebb Musical; Kiss of the Spider Woman*. Films: *Cabaret; Lucky Lady; NY, NY; Funny Lady; Kramer vs. Kramer; A Matter of Time; Places in the Heart; French Postcards; Stepping Out*. Television: "Liza with a Z" (Liza Minnelli), "Goldie and Liza Together" (With Goldie Hawn), "Ol' Blue Eyes is Back," "Baryshnikov on Broadway," "An Early Frost," "Liza in London." Upcoming: *The Skin of Our Teeth*.

CONTENTS

TITLE   PAGE NO.

Rita's Theme 4

Willing To Ride 6

girl — Second Chance 14
verse #1 only
Dance With Me 19

The Last Girl 24

girl — Everybody's Girl 30

duet 2x girls — Wet 39

Lovebird 48

Somebody Older 53

First You Dream 57

Steel Pier 68

RITA'S THEME

Lyrics by
FRED EBB

Music by
JOHN KANDER

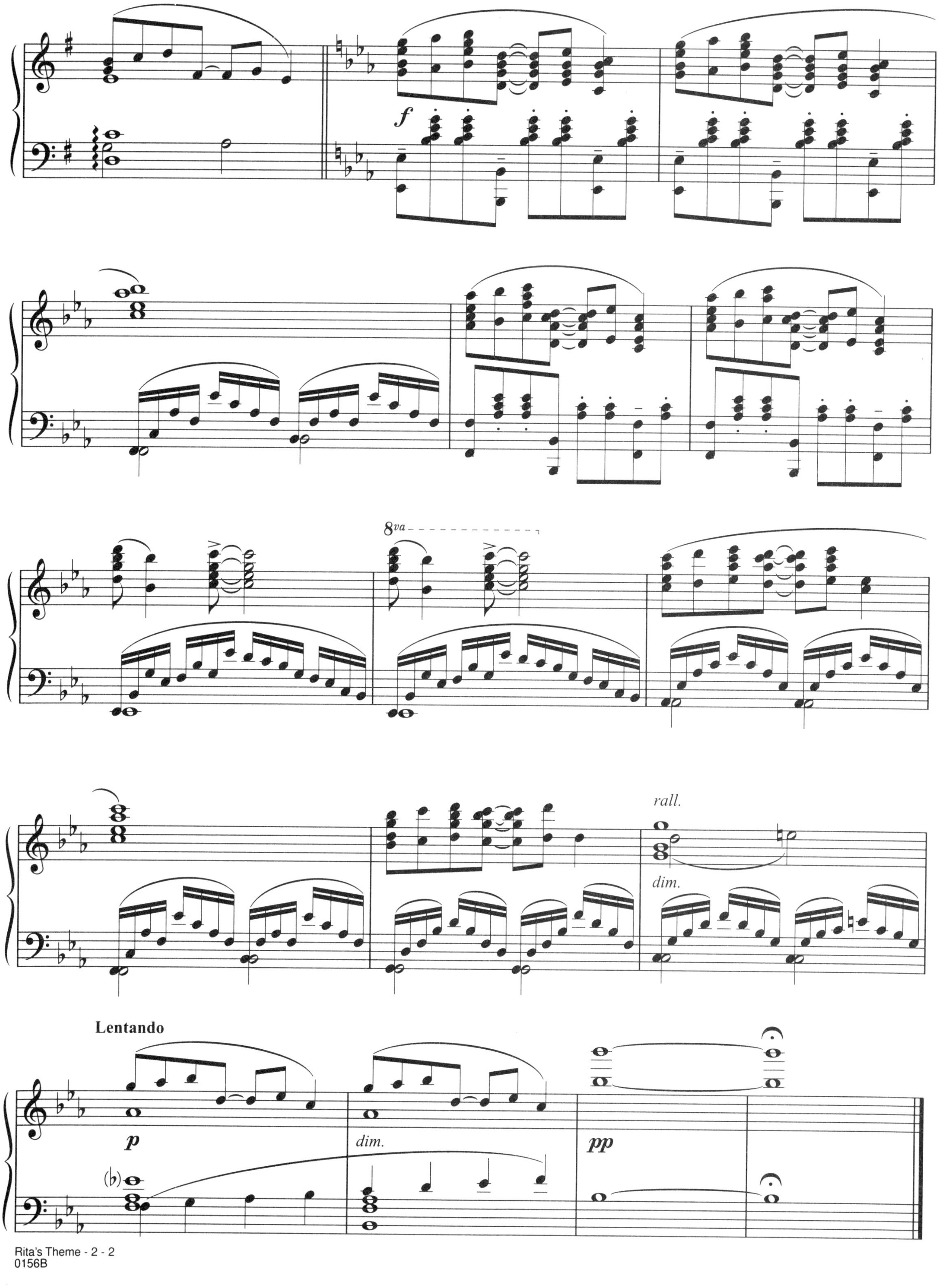
f
8va
rall.
dim.
Lentando
p
(♭)
dim.
pp

WILLING TO RIDE

Lyrics by
FRED EBB

Music by
JOHN KANDER

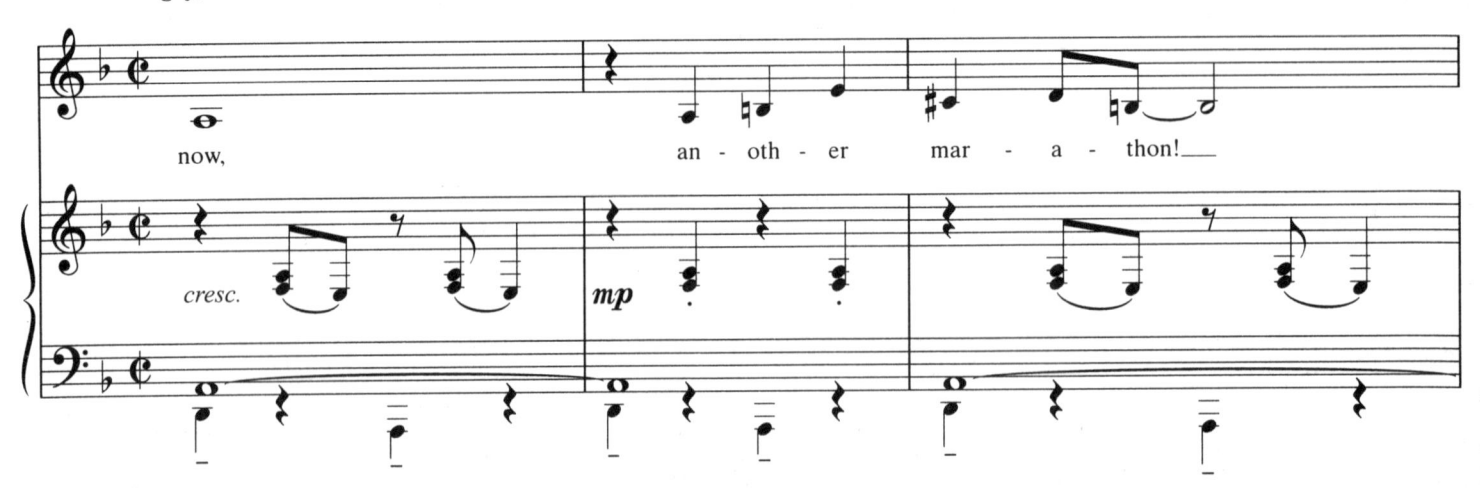

Easy waltz

Twelve Ocean Drive, right by the shore. Not many rooms, I only count four. But for

Angry, with drive

now, another marathon!

Willing to Ride - 8 - 1
0156B

© 1997 KANDER & EBB, INC. (BMI)
All Rights Administered by WARNER-TAMERLANE PUBLISHING CORP.
All Rights Reserved

Another dead on my feet! Another time clock to beat, bruise on my shin, des-p'rate to win, just like it's always been.

cresc. poco a poco

rall.

Tempo I

Twelve Ocean Drive,

accel. poco a poco

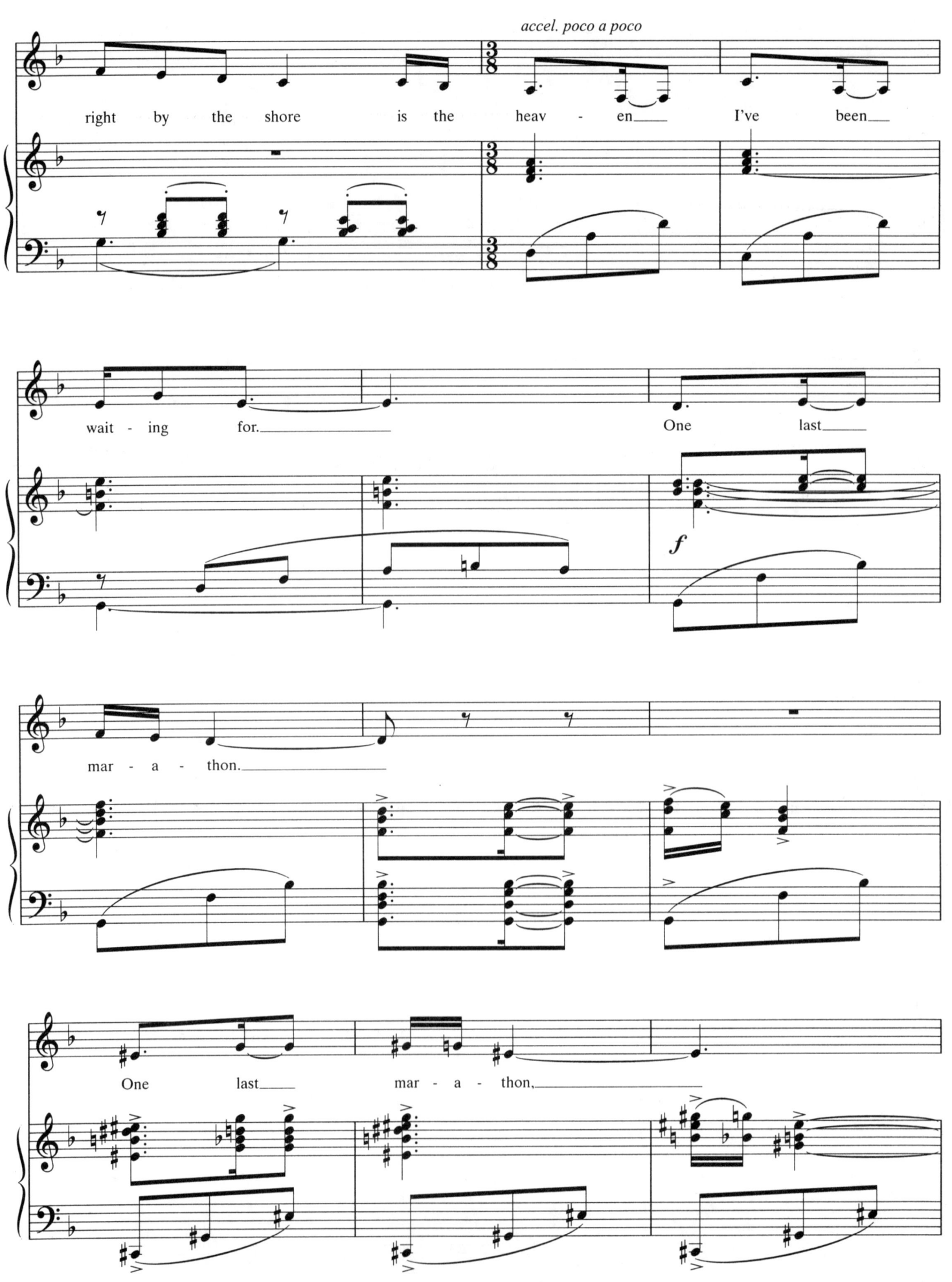

right by the shore is the heav-en I've been wait-ing for. One last mar-a-thon. One last mar-a-thon, just one more.

dim. *mp* *cresc. poco a poco*

poco rit. **Tempo I**

Here I go a- gain. I can hear that mer-ry-go-round, and though I nev-er cared much for the sound, I'm will-ing to ride.

mf *cresc.*

There's the fer-ris wheel, a mir-a-cle, a cir-cle of steel. It's fun-ny how ner-vous it's mak-ing me feel, yet will-ing to ride. This time, al-though, I'll do it!

11

but - ter - fly ri - ot in - side. I'm will - ing to

A Tempo
(Instrumental)
ride.

(Sung)
But now must be now and then must be then. I've

struck out be - fore and I could - n't for - get if I tried.

13

But I'm up to bat a-gain, toss-ing my hat a-gain. Here I go a-gain, will-ing to ride.

cresc. poco a poco

a tempo

ff

sfz

Willing to Ride - 8 - 8
0156B

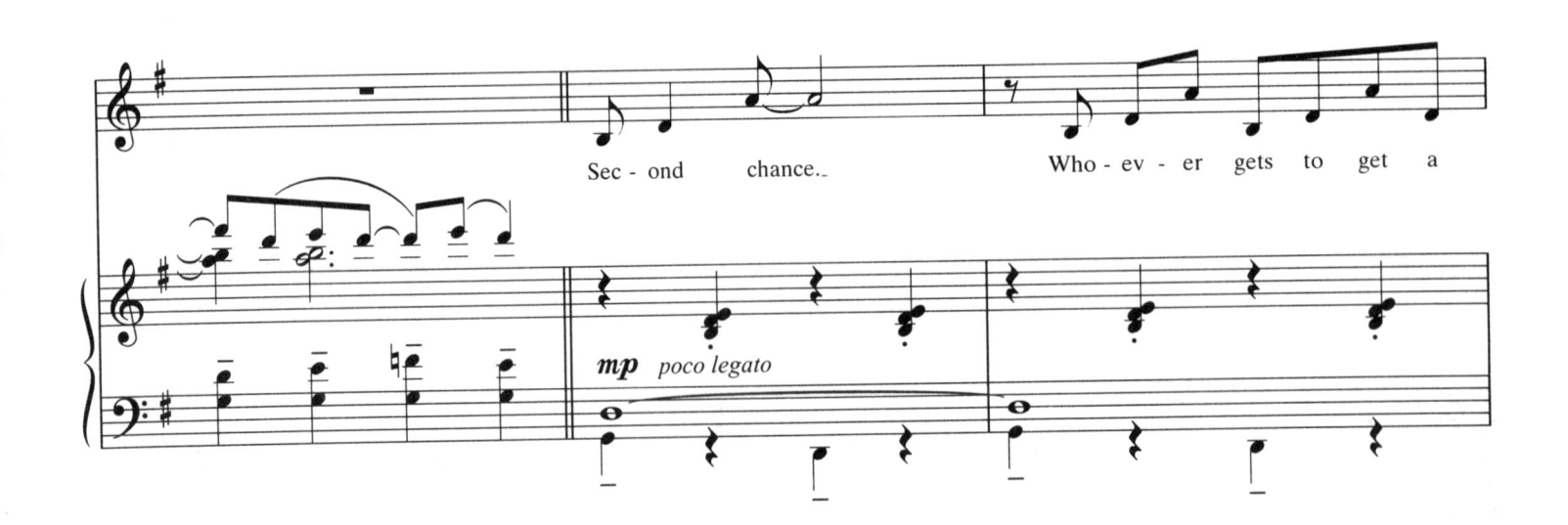

SECOND CHANCE

Lyrics by
FRED EBB

Music by
JOHN KANDER

Tell me that!
f
marcato
One more try.
mp
poco legato
Who-ev-er gets to get an-oth-er try?
Who-ev-er gets to sing the big re-prise?
cresc.
Tell me, please.
mf
Once you're down, You're

down, they say. Once you're out, you're out to stay. No one tells you you can get right up and you can start all o-ver with a sec-ond chance. When-ev-er life has gone from bad to worse,_ you've got to run your movie in re-verse._ Re-re-hearse._ Soon that curse_ will dis-perse._ But first you've got to get___ a sec-ond chance.___

To Coda ⊕

A sec - ond chance.

DANCE WITH ME

Lyrics by
FRED EBB

Music by
JOHN KANDER

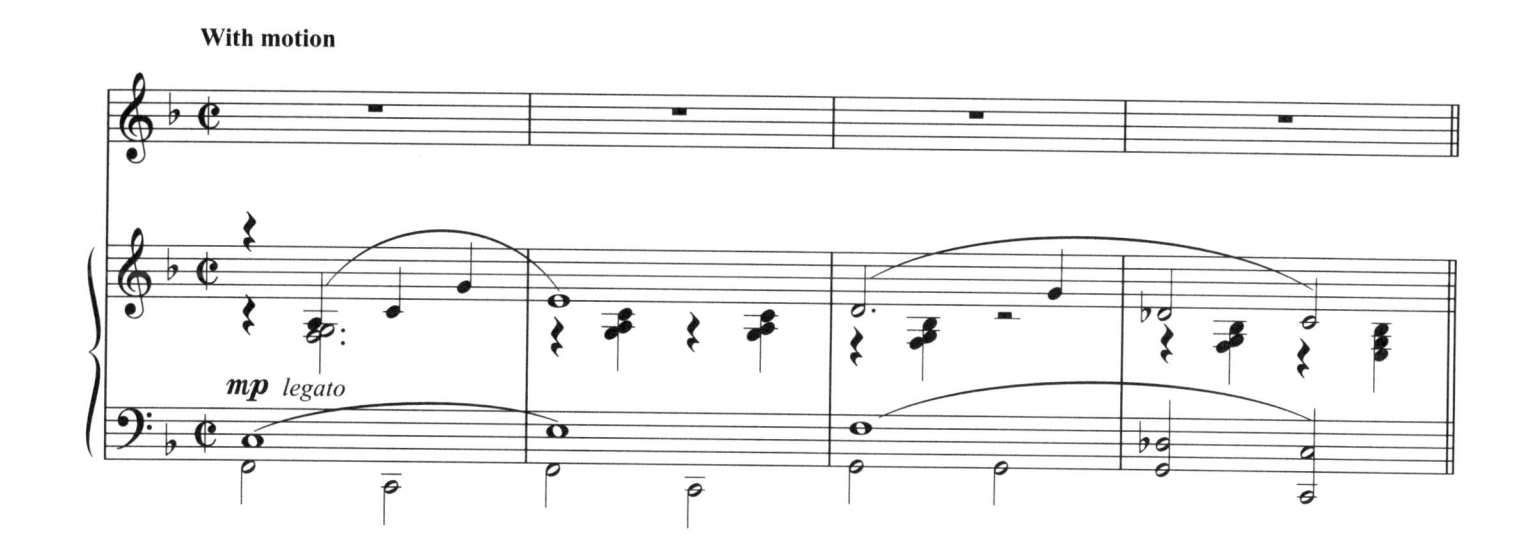

With motion

Dance with me, Dance with me.

Hold me as we cross the floor.

Dance with Me - 5 - 1
0156B

© 1997 KANDER & EBB, INC. (BMI)
All Rights Administered by WARNER-TAMERLANE PUBLISHING CORP.
All Rights Reserved

Light as air, what a pair!

Tell me could heav-en be an-y-thing more?

Whirl a-round, twirl a-round, fol-low me and soon you'll see Fred and A-dele nev-er glid-ed as well____ as we do when you dance

with me.

Dance with me, dance with me,

hold me as we cross the floor.____

Light as air, what a pair!

Tell me could heav-en be an-y-thing more?

Whirl a-round, twirl a-round,

fol-low me and soon you'll see

Fred and A-dele___ nev-er glid-ed as well___ as we do when you dance with me.

THE LAST GIRL

Lyrics by
FRED EBB

Music by
JOHN KANDER

Flowing, with motion

The last girl _____ I'll ev - er love is o - ver there, _____

The Last Girl - 6 - 1
0156B

© 1997 KANDER & EBB, INC. (BMI)
All Rights Administered by WARNER-TAMERLANE PUBLISHING CORP.
All Rights Reserved

danc - ing in some - one else - 's arms. The last girl I'll care a - bout is o - ver there, ob -

li-vi-ous, it's clear, of some-one stand-ing here. She daz-zles like a mir-ror in the sun. She

must be my re - ward for some - thing
won - der - ful I've done.
dim.
The
mp
last girl I'll ev - er love walked
in my life.
The

mo - ment was strict - ly un - re -
hearsed. But The
cresc.
rall. poco a poco
last girl I'll ev - er love is
o - ver there. And the

A bit slower
last girl, it's a - maz - ing! The last girl,
it's as - tound - ing! The last girl turns
out to be the first.
p
pp

EVERYBODY'S GIRL

Lyrics by
FRED EBB

Music by
JOHN KANDER

drove a man wild un-til he was out of con-trol. I tru-ly be-lieve that

I am a mod - ern day Car - men.
In spite of the fact I
do not "ha - bla es - pag - nol,"
that
p
sfz
Poco rubato
girl was ex - act - ly like me.
mp colla voce

Con poco moto
We share this phi - lo - so - phy. O -
cresc.
le, I say. I'm
f
not the type who's read - y for dat - in' some - one stead - y. I'm ev - 'ry - bod - y's girl.
mp poco marcato
3
On Sun - day night, it's Dan - ny, on Mon - day, may - be Man - ny. I'm

ev - 'ry - bod - y's girl.
There's a point to my be -
hav - ior which is: smart girls al - ways share their rich - es.
So if your heart suc - cumbs don't let it, you're cer - tain to re - gret it. All
oth - ers, come and get it!
I'm ev - 'ry - bod - y's girl.
cresc.
f
mf
cresc.
f
sfz

With more kick
(Spoken:)
I could never be a cowhand's girl.
8va
ff
molto marcato
(Sung:)
La la la la la la.
(Spoken:)
And do you wanna know why?
(8va)
p
ff
ENSEMBLE:
SHELBY:
(Spoken:)
(Sung:)
Why?
'Cause I just can't keep my calves together.
I'm
ev-'ry-bod-y's girl.
Some old Greek called A-ri-sto-tle said it:
mp
cresc.

If you got it, why not spread it? So don't go rattling any sabres, exerting any labors, just share me with the neighbors! I'm ev-'ry-bod-y's girl. In

37

And so to re-af-firm my sta-tus, it's ab-sol-ut-ly grat-is to use my ap-par-a-tus. I'm ev-ry-bod-y's girl.

(Spoken:) Men and me are like pianos:
When they get upright, I feel grand.

Ev-'ry-bod-y's girl.

WET

Lyrics by
FRED EBB

Music by
JOHN KANDER

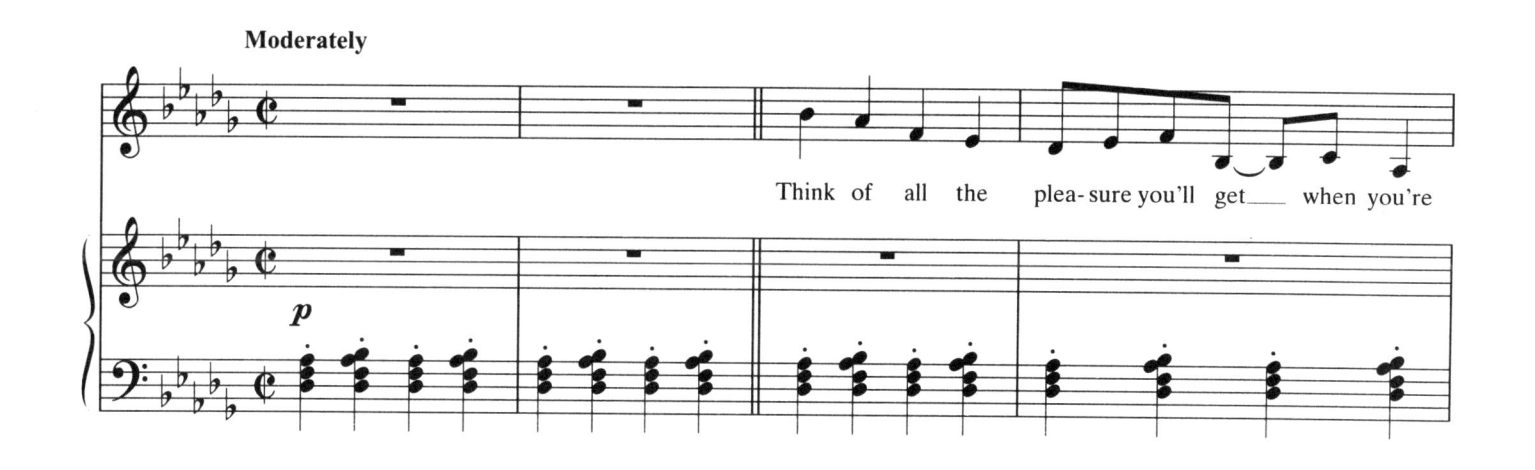

having barrels of cash. But I believe that being happy is here a splash. There a splash.

Let's get ready, set, and begin to be all wet.

Feel that water lapping your skin when you're all wet. Come

on, let's be a cou-ple of sports._ Show your nerve and show your shorts._

There's no time for jok-ing._ This night could be smok-ing_

once we both get soak - in' wet.

Pa - pa nev - er taught me to swim.

Think of all the plea-sure you'll get___ when you're all wet.

So right now I'm fum - ing at him.

Not a trou - ble you can't for - get___ when you're all wet.

43

Wa - ter games, well, I've nev - er been to them,
Some folks say that be - ing hap - py is hav - ing bar - rels of cash. But

But she could be talk - ing me in - to them.
I be - lieve that be - ing hap - py is here a splash. There a splash.

If I sink and
Let's get rea - dy, set, and be - gin to be

Wet - 9 - 5
0156B

start to go down,_____ in her arms, a
all wet. Feel that wa-ter lap-ping your skin_____ when you're

nice way to drown._____ All right here I go,
all wet. Come on, let's be a cou-ple of sports._____

watch out down be-low._____ All the rules are bro-ken_____
Show your nerve and show your shorts._ All the rules are bro-ken_____

Wet - 9 - 6
0156B

when the fire is smok-in'.___ Douse it get-ting soak - in'

wet.

wet.

Come

Come

on, get rea-dy, then let's go___ plunge in-to that H-2-0!___

Noth-ing need be spo - ken.___ All ta-boos are bro - ken___

once we two get soak - in'___

47

wet.

wet.

Why be feel-ing fran-tic when you

Why be feel-ing fran-tic when you

could be all ro-man-tic hav-ing fun in the At-lan-tic get-ting soak-in' wet?!

could be all ro-man-tic hav-ing fun in the At-lan-tic get-ting soak-in' wet?!

LOVEBIRD

Lyrics by
FRED EBB

Music by
JOHN KANDER

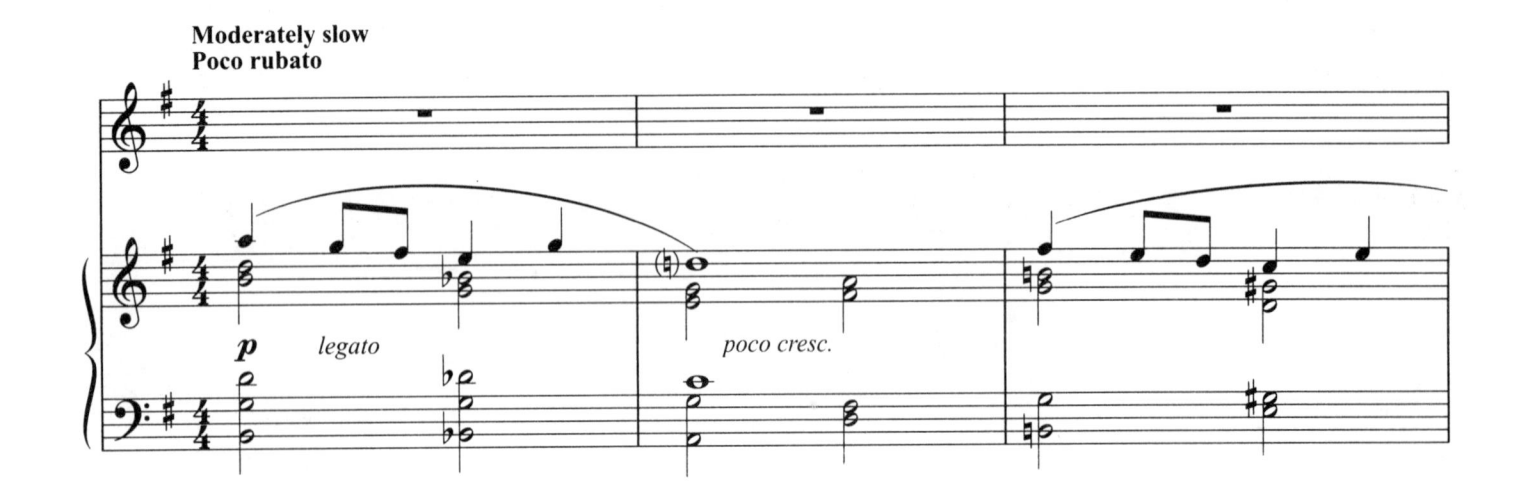

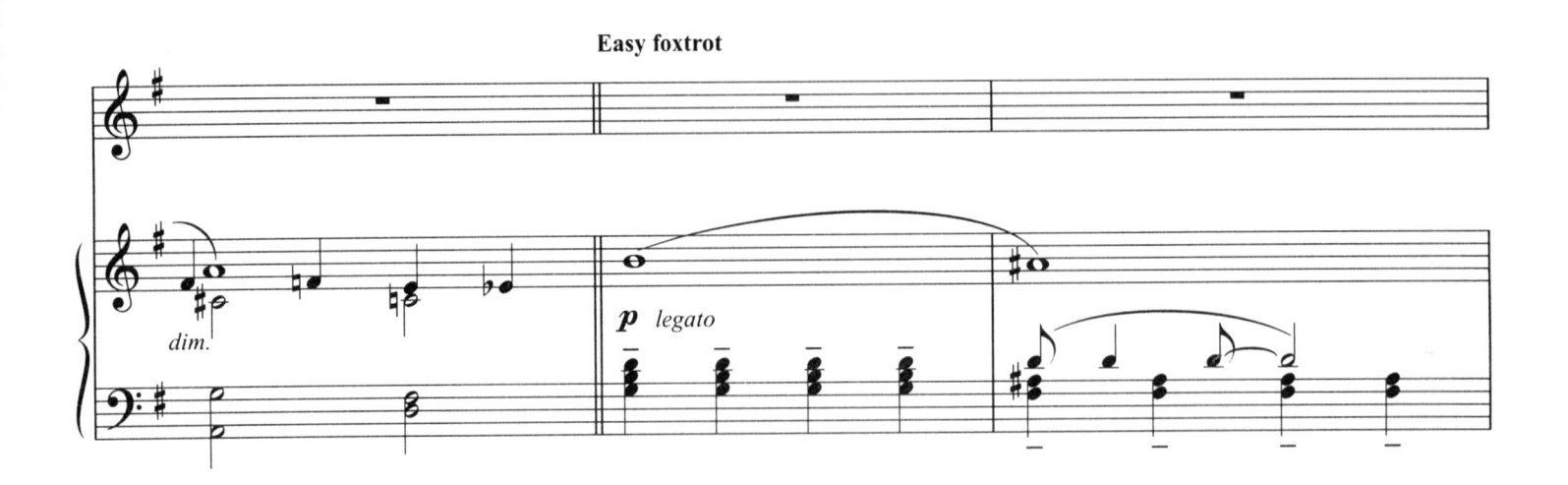

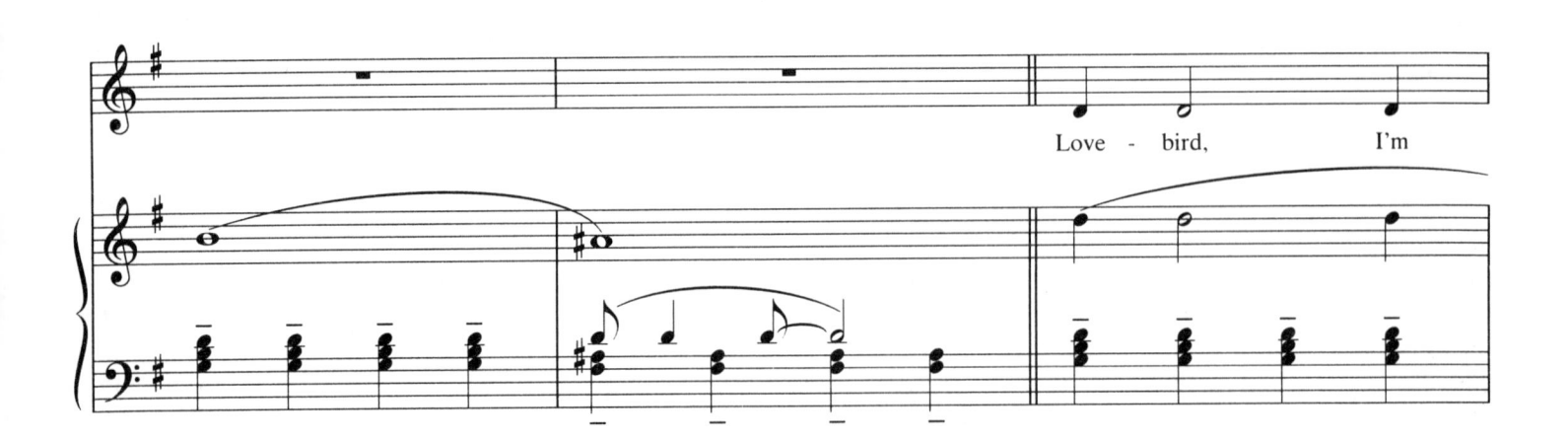

Moderately slow
Poco rubato

p legato   *poco cresc.*

Easy foxtrot

dim.   *p legato*

Love- bird,   I'm

Lovebird - 5 - 1
0156B

feel-ing blue. Love-bird, we should be two.

How can we have love-seed to grow, when I'm a-lone and

poco cresc.

poco rall. *a tempo*

feel-ing so low, so - lo? Love-bird, come

dim.

on, be there. Love-bird, let's make a pair. If

sim.

you stay a-way from the world I'm dream-ing of,

I'll be a love-bird with no one to love.

Nobody buys one shoe. Nobody wants one glove.

Some things nat-u-ral-ly come with a mate. That's why I'm cry-ing when I state:

poco rall. **With a little motion**

Love-bird, come on, be there. Love-bird, let's make a pair. If you stay a-way from the world I'm dream-ing of,

Poco rubato

I'll be a love-bird, a lone-ly love-bird with no one to love.

SOMEBODY OLDER

Lyrics by
FRED EBB

Music by
JOHN KANDER

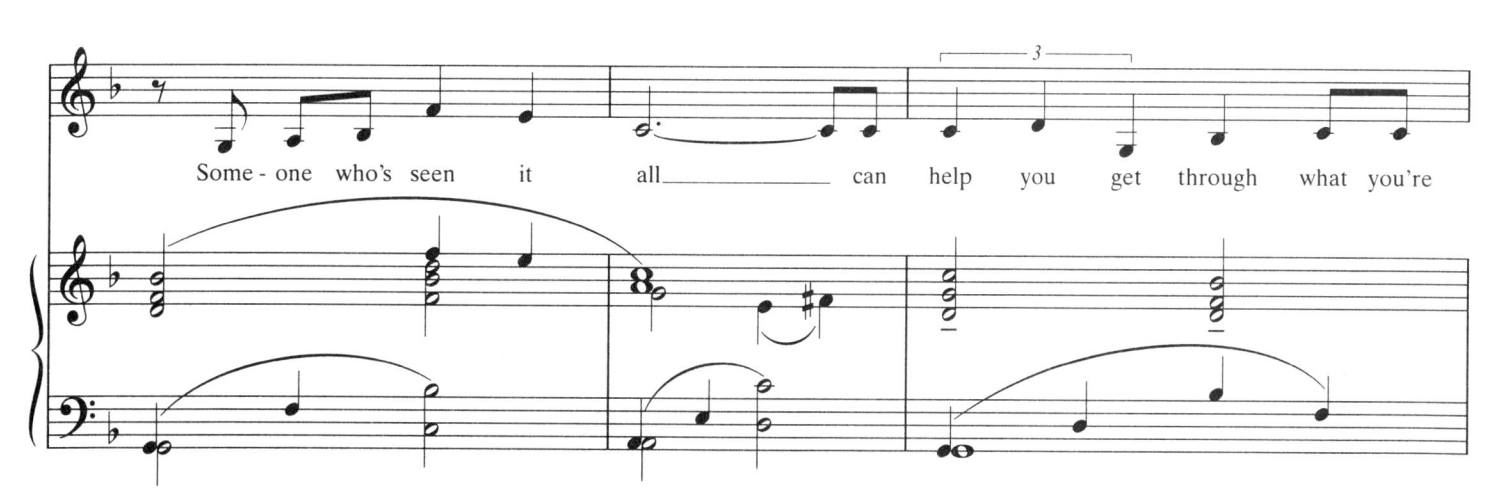

Moderately slow

Some-bod-y old-er can teach you things. Some-bod-y old-er can show you how.

Some-one who's seen it all ___ can help you get through what you're

Somebody Older - 4 - 1
0156B

© 1997 KANDER & EBB, INC. (BMI)
All Rights Administered by WARNER-TAMERLANE PUBLISHING CORP.
All Rights Reserved

go - ing through now. Some - bod - y wis - er who's been a - round can pro - ba - bly send you safe - ly on your way. Lis - ten and hear what some - bod - y old - er might say. Some - one who'd pro - ba - bly be some-one a lot like me.

Some-bod-y wis-er who's been a-round_____ Can

pro - ba - bly send you safe - ly on your way. Some - bod - y young needs some - bod - y old - er, it's clear. Some - one who'd pro - ba - bly be some - one a lot like me.

First You Dream

Lyrics by
FRED EBB

Music by
JOHN KANDER

Con moto, poco rubato

First you dream, dream about incredible things.

Then you look and sud-den-ly you have wings. You can fly. You can fly. But first you dream.

accel.
cresc. poco a poco
mf
dim.
p
cresc.

First you dream, dream about remarkable times.

Close your eyes and see how your spirit climbs. You can fly, you can soar. Feel the wind, hear it roar. It's easy now, imagine that. But first you dream.

Here we are,_____ high a-bove the roof-tops._____ There's a barn,

there's a field of corn. And that little white house where an-other you was born. Isn't it fine? Isn't it fair being up here, looking down there?

Take my hand, I prom-ise that I won't let you fall.

Don't look back, the look-ing back could end it all. Off we go

to the sky.
Straight a -
head,
you and I.
To - geth - er now,
to -
geth - er now,
but first things first.

First you dream.

Off we go to the sky. Straight ahead, you and I. To-

67

geth - er now,_____ to - geth - er now,_____

but first things first._____ First you dream._____

dim. poco a poco

First you dream._____

rall. poco a poco

dim.

pp

First You Dream - 11 - 11
0156B

STEEL PIER

Lyrics by
FRED EBB

Music by
JOHN KANDER

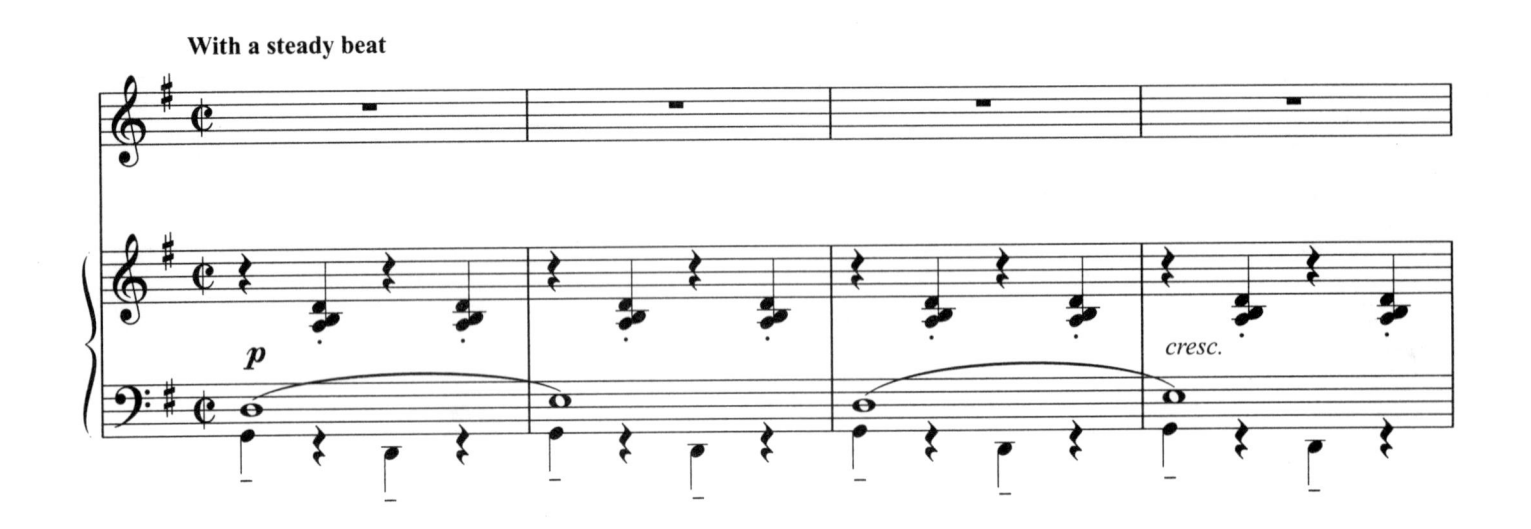

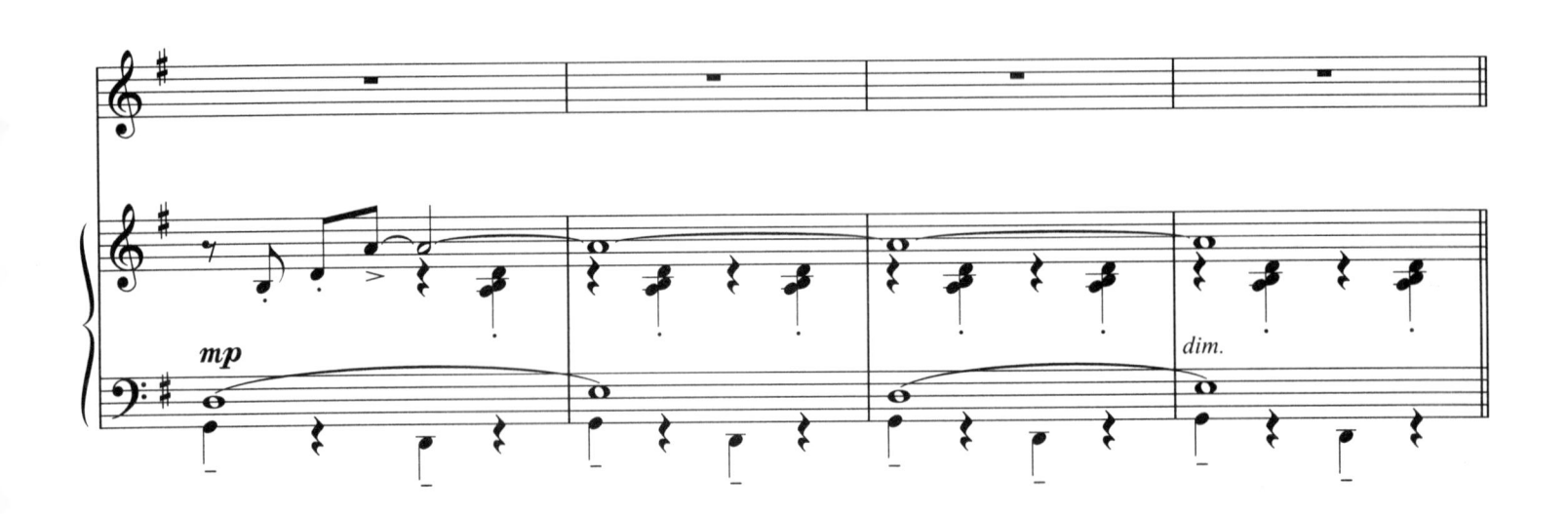

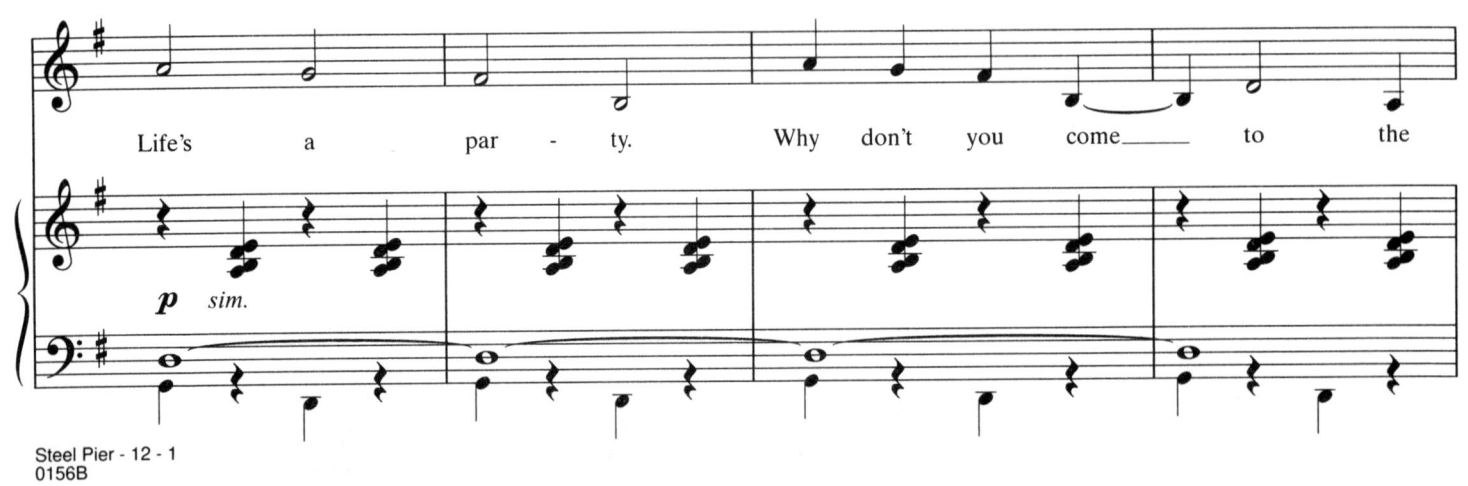

With a steady beat

Life's a par- ty. Why don't you come to the

Steel Pier - 12 - 1
0156B

© 1997 KANDER & EBB, INC. (BMI)
All Rights Administered by WARNER-TAMERLANE PUBLISHING CORP.
All Rights Reserved

Steel Pier?

No one's ever gloom-y or glum at the Steel Pier.

Dip your toes in-to the o-cean.

Rub a lit-tle sun-tan lo-tion.

Pay your dough and ride all the rides.

Sit on the board-walk watch-ing the tides.

Steel Pier - 12 - 4
0156B

No place draws a friendlier crowd than the Steel-Pier. So watch the joy go on and on, like some daffy ma - ra - thon. Bring your troubles here, watch them dis - a - pear at the tru - ly up - roar - i - ous, glam - our - ous, glo - ri - ous Steel Pier.

L'istesso tempo

Life's a par - ty.

Why don't you come to the Steel Pier?

No one's ever gloom-y or glum at the Steel Pier. Dip your toes in- to the o- cean. Rub a lit- tle

sun - tan lo - tion. Pay your dough, be

will - ing to ride. Sit on the board - walk

watch - ing the tides.

All Atlantic City is proud of the Steel Pier.

No place draws a friendlier crowd than the Steel Pier. So

watch the joy go on and on,____
Like this cra - zy mar - a - thon.____
Bring your trou - bles here. Watch them dis - ap - pear at the
tru - ly up - roar - i - ous, glam - o - rous, glor - i - ous

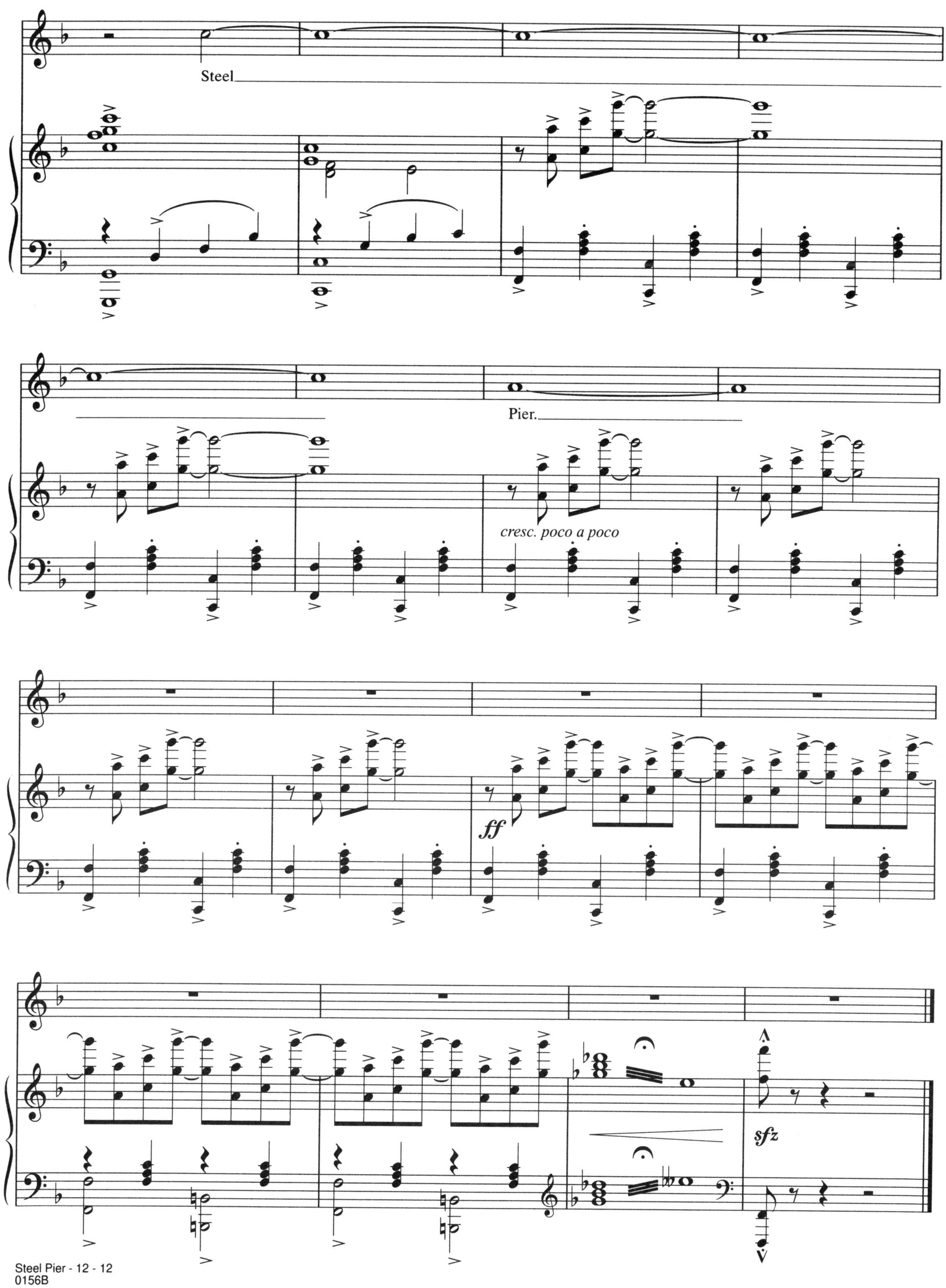
Steel
Pier.
cresc. poco a poco
ff
sfz

Artwork courtesy Serino Coyne

Steel Pier Logo Photography:
Ray Herbert Archives; Arnette Webster Riding Red Lipps, photograph courtesy Arnette Webster French; Marathon Photos from the book *Atlantic City: 125 Years of Ocean Madness* by Vicki Gold Levi and Lee Eisenberg